Zen for Kids

50+ MINDFUL ACTIVITIES AND STORIES
to Shine Loving-Kindness in the World

Laura Burges
Illustrated by **Melissa Iwai**

bala kids

For David, always.

Each of you is perfect the way you are...
and you can use a little improvement.

—SHUNRYU SUZUKI ROSHI

CONTENTS

A Word to Parents

When Shambhala Publications invited me to write a book about Zen for kids, I wasn't sure it was such a great idea. I've been a member of the San Francisco Zen Center for a long time, and my daughter, Nova, and many other children have grown up in our community. We don't indoctrinate our children into Zen Buddhism or expect them to subscribe to a set of beliefs. If Zen does call to them at some point, we want them to have the freedom to make that choice themselves, should their lives present it to them. We hope our daily activity, the way we live and treat other people, will illuminate Zen practice to ourselves and others and speak for itself.

But then I thought about the special place we make for children in our sangha, our Zen community. They join us in silence at the beginning of our community meals. We include them in celebrations to honor the changing of the seasons. We have Family Day, the first Sunday of each month, at Green Gulch Farm in Marin County, California. On that day, families come to the first part of the Sunday lecture and then disperse for activities in the garden. In the fall, we have a special Sejiki Ceremony, a traditional Zen Buddhist event that honors the ancestors and the unseen spirits of the world. At this ceremony, in the Buddha Hall, we make offerings of food and good wishes to departed loved ones; we chant and make rowdy noises and acknowledge the "hungry ghosts," the unsatisfied spirits of other realms and our own restless states of mind and body. Families come in costume, as we would at a Purim festival or on Halloween night.

I began to look more deeply at the ways we nurture children in our community. I also wanted to find ways to extend their experience in the sangha with practice-related stories and activities. How can we benefit our own children, and the children beyond our sangha, with fun, kid-friendly explorations?

My intention is that this book will enrich children's lives with this spirit of inclusion, offering timeless stories and engaging practices for kids to do within the warm circle of family life. You might want to do some of the practices along with your children; you might want to read the stories aloud together and talk about what they mean to you. Then again, there may be things that your children will want to explore on their own.

Zen flowered in East Asia and has traveled all over the world. Because Zen's spirit is universal, I've chosen to retell stories from several different traditions that point to the spirit of Zen. I hope that these pages are a welcome addition to your family life. Please use the stories and activities in any way that works for you and your children. You may want to revisit them from time to time, since children will benefit from them in different ways as they grow and change.

Zazen Practice

The heart of Zen practice is *zazen*—Zen meditation. In a Zen community, members gather in the temple *zendo* (meditation hall) in the morning and evening to sit zazen with one another. We enter and find our seat, whether on a cushion—or *zafu*, in Japanese—or in a chair. We bow toward our sitting place to honor all those who have gone before us and to recognize and honor the practice of sitting and our own awakened nature. Then we turn in a clockwise direction and bow toward the assembly. We settle ourselves, sitting cross-legged on the zafu or upright in the chair, facing the wall, and listen for the three bells that begin the meditation session.

We sit with our spine straight and our lower back strong. Our shoulders are rolled back, our eyes slightly open, with a diffuse awareness. Our hands rest in our lap, palms facing up. We use the "cosmic mudra," our left palm resting on our right palm, with our thumb tips lightly touching, forming an oval. It helps to imagine that we have a string lifting us up from the crown of our head, with our chin tucked in a bit. Our tongue rests on the back of our front teeth. Our ears are in line with our shoulders and our nose is in line with our navel. We take a few deep breaths and then allow our breath to assume its natural rhythm, not trying to control it in any way, but just observing it. We can help focus on our breath by breathing in and then out through our nose; breathe in, then out, counting mentally "one"; in, then out, counting "two"; and so on, up to ten, and then begin again. When our mind wanders, we gently come back to our breath. We sit with no idea of achieving anything, just sitting quietly with our breath. When the bell rings to signal the end of zazen, we bow in a particular way, called *gassho* in Japanese: We press our flattened palms together, fingers aligned, in front of our heart and our elbows lifted slightly, and we bend a little at our waist.

While it is helpful to sit and practice with others, we can also sit on our own, in our own homes. In the zendo, periods of sitting are usually forty minutes long, with ten minutes of slow walking meditation in between periods. At home, of course, you can determine how long you might want to sit. For children, short periods of two or five or ten minutes are more appropriate.

This classic way of sitting zazen in such a formal way can be challenging for children. A guided meditation at home with the family can help them focus. While children might feel self-conscious or a little embarrassed at first, I've found from using these practices as a classroom teacher that they can come to enjoy silence and stillness. It will be helpful to your children, to your whole family, if you develop a sitting practice of your own. Thich Nhat Hanh, the Vietnamese priest and peace activist, says, "If we are peaceful, if we are happy, we can smile, and everyone in our family, our entire society, will benefit from our peace." This is an important reminder. We don't just claim peace and happiness as our birthright; rather, we rest in happiness and peace for the benefit of all beings.

A Family Meditation

Family members can take turns leading this guided meditation. It will be helpful for you to have a bowl-like meditation bell on hand to ring at the beginning and end of zazen. Children who are able to read will enjoy being the guide now and then. These phrases can be read slowly and calmly by the guide while the other family members hold them in mind for a few moments and then gently let them go. The guide should take a few calm breaths in between each sentence. Of course, you can adapt these words to the needs and identity of your family.

Begin by ringing your meditation bell three times. Then the guide says:

* "I sit upright, leaning to neither the left nor the right."
* "I enjoy the feeling of the air entering and leaving my body."
* "I can feel my chest and belly rising and falling when I breathe."
* "I let go of any worry and feel peace settling in my body."
* "I feel my whole body, awake and alive in this moment."
* "I can feel my heart opening with kindness, like a rose."
* "I feel at home in the life of my family."
* "I feel connected to all beings, past, present, and future."
* "I am ready to find gentleness and bravery within myself."

Family members can continue to sit for a few minutes after these words are spoken. End by ringing the bell once. Then the family members gassho. Once your children are comfortable doing a guided meditation a few times, they will be better able to sit in silence for a few minutes at a time, just breathing, without words.

Another simple family practice is just to stop together before you all leave home for the day, ring your meditation bell, and take three deep breaths with one another. This can increase your sense of intention, as a family, to bring peace with you out into the world.

A Home Altar

Many people like to create a home altar—a shelf or space that can be a focal point for your family. You can cover your altar with a pretty cloth and add a candle, an image of the Buddha or other inspiring figures, and some flowers. If you go for a family walk and find a feather, a shell, or a pretty leaf, your children will enjoy putting them on the altar. You can also have photographs of friends or family members who have died and whom you want to always remember. Your meditation bell can sit on your altar and members of the family can ring it to encourage a calm moment or at the beginning of a family meeting or mealtime.

This book springs from my own Zen practice and from my experience teaching children and raising my daughter, Nova; any errors or omissions are my own. It is not meant to be the "last word" on Buddhism and Zen but rather a beginning. The ancient stories that I have chosen to reimagine are the ones that speak to me, and I have had fun playing with genders, species, and plots to make the stories more accessible for today's readers. I hope you and your children enjoy reading and talking about them as you go along.

The rest of this book is addressed to your children, and I have indicated instances where adult guidance will be needed. Perhaps the most important thing I can say is to let your child take the lead. If they don't feel like taking up an activity, please honor that and put it aside for another time. Children shouldn't be forced to meditate or to talk about uncomfortable or private feelings unless and until they want to.

I hope your family enjoys this book as much as I have enjoyed creating it for you.

May all beings be happy; may they be joyous and live in safety.

Laura Burges

You can help your child prepare for the activities
in this book by providing:

* a meditation bell, available online or in stores that
  carry spiritual supplies
* a kitchen timer
* art supplies, such as watercolors, colored pencils,
  and markers
* a home altar (see page ix)
* chairs and/or zafus (cushions) for meditation
* a glitter jar (see chapter 3)
* a journal for your child to record drawings,
  thoughts, and feelings

Introduction

Have you ever heard the word *Zen*? It's a Japanese word that's fun to say because it has a kind of zingy sound, like an arrow whizzing past your ear. Zen is what happens when you sit quietly, noticing your breath and what it feels like just to be alive. We are often so busy doing things and thinking things and wanting things that we don't always notice that we are alive! Taking some time to sit quietly might change how we treat other people and how we act in the world. Here are some moments of Zen:

I taught third grade and, once upon a time, there was a boy in my class named Nathan. One day, as he was walking by my desk, he suddenly stopped and did a little dance. I called him over and whispered, "Nathan, what were you thinking about just then?" And he said to me, excited, "Laura! Do you ever forget you are alive and all of a sudden you remember?" That was a moment of Zen.

There was a girl in my class named Elena. I asked the third-graders what superpower they would like to have. One student said, "I'd like to be invisible!" Another said, "I'd like to be a shapeshifter!" And Elena said, "I'd like the superpower of being able to understand other people's feelings!" That was a moment of Zen.

There was a boy in my class named Ian. He liked to play with the other kids during recess. But sometimes he liked to sit quietly on the bench outside and look at the clouds and watch the wind rippling through the poplar trees. Those were moments of Zen.

There was a boy in my class named Paul. One day, I said something you've probably heard grown-ups say: "Great minds think alike." Paul thought for a moment and said, "No, they don't! That's what makes them great!" That was a moment of Zen.

Zen is a way of living and of looking at the world, and it is a part of the way of life known as Buddhism. This way of looking at the world starts with what we call a "practice," the practice of just sitting still for a little while and remembering that we are alive. The Japanese word for this is also fun to say—*zazen*. Another zingy word! *Zazen* means "just sitting," which is a way to describe Zen meditation.

When we are "just sitting" it seems like we aren't doing much, just being alive. But then we get up and we live in the world. How do we want to treat other people? How do we want to take care of ourselves, plants, animals, and the things that we use every day? How do we want to speak up and stand up for ourselves and others? What special gifts do we have to offer this world? Does what we do make a difference? I think it does!

Here is a story about Bellen Woodard. She saw that the world needed something and decided to do something about it.

When Bellen was ten years old, she was the only African American student in her class. One day, another student asked her for the "skin-colored crayon." Bellen knew that the other student meant the "peach-colored crayon" because she had been hearing that for a long time. She thought about it, and she decided that the next time someone said "the skin-colored crayon," she would respond, "Which color do you mean? Because that could be any number of colors." Bellen had an idea. She decided to start the More Than Peach Project. Her goal is to get boxes of multicultural crayons to students whose skin comes in all shades, so everyone can learn to love and appreciate one another and their differences. With the help of lots of donations, she is well on her way to sending out eighty thousand boxes of these colorful crayons, so kids can see that there are more skin colors than just peach! Bellen calls herself "the first crayon activist." Each of us has special gifts to give the world, and Bellen has found one of hers. What do you think your special gifts will be?

The Three Treasures in Buddhism are Buddha, Dharma, and Sangha. They are called "treasures" because they are so special. *Buddha* reminds us that each of us can wake up and enjoy our life and help other people. *Dharma* is the word for his teachings, for everyday truth. And *Sangha* is our deep connection to one another, to the plants and animals around us, and to the whole universe. I hope this book will help you get to know the Three Treasures a little better.

I have spent many years teaching children and practicing Zen. In this book, I collect and retell some stories that remind me of the Zen way of life. Stories about being kind, about learning to be patient and giving, about being brave and gentle. Stories about how we are all connected to one another and to life. Stories about what it feels like to do your best and to do the right thing. I hope you enjoy these stories and that you will try some of the practices that come along with them. These activities, like the one below, will help bring these words and ideas to life. The glossary at the end of the book will help explain words that may be new to you.

Decorating Your Own Personal Journal

We can learn a lot about ourselves and our world by writing down or drawing our thoughts and feelings. It will be helpful for you to have your own special journal where you can record some of your memories, ideas, poems, and drawings. Ask a grown-up to help you find a good journal with lined pages and a sturdy cover. Take some family photographs, cut out some pictures from magazines, or make some shapes with colored paper to glue on the cover, along with your name. Before you write your thoughts or feelings for that day, write the date at the top of the page. You can also ask someone to help you with writing things down, if you need to. Later, when you look back and read your journal, it will feel like reading stories about your own life!

JUST SITTING
...
JUST BREATHING

Buddhism began with one man, who sat down quietly under a tree in India. When he stood up, he began to teach, and his teaching spread from country to country. He is called the Buddha, which means "one who has awakened." This is his story.

Story: A Boy Named Siddhartha

A very long time ago, a boy named Siddhartha Gautama was born in a country that is now called Nepal, north of India. His family was very wealthy, and he had everything his heart could wish for—beautiful clothes, delicious food, a wonderful palace to live in, and many servants to take care of his every need. His parents wanted to protect him from any sadness, so when he would go out of the palace gates and into the villages, his father would tell a servant, "Quick, run ahead of my son's carriage to make sure that the boy never sees anyone who is sick, who is old, who is dying!"

One day, Siddhartha wanted to see for himself what the world was like. He dressed as a humble servant and climbed over the palace walls. He wandered through the crowded streets of nearby villages and saw people who were very poor. When he saw a woman who was terribly sick, lying in the shade of a tree, he didn't know what to think. He had never seen a sick person before. Then he saw a man bent over, with long gray hair and a gray beard, walking with a cane. "Who can this be, and what is wrong with him?" he thought, for he had never seen anyone who was old.

Then he saw a family gathered around a woman lying on a wooden cot with fragrant flowers heaped on top of her. Some of the people were crying. The woman didn't move, and it was clear that her life was over.

"I see now," Siddhartha thought, "that this life is precious and that one day my life, too, will come to an end. No one is excused from the truth of sickness, old age, and death!"

And then Siddhartha saw a wandering holy person, a *sadhu*—someone who had left behind the comforts of the world to seek truth and freedom. Now the boy knew that there were other people like himself in the world, people who wanted to understand the mysteries of life.

He also knew now, because he had seen for himself, that there is terrible suffering in the world. When he was old enough, he left home to find out the cause of this suffering. Sadly he left behind his young wife and his son. He cut off his hair and found some friends who had also left home to find the truth, and they traveled from place to place together, carrying their begging bowls with them and sleeping on the ground.

Siddhartha had lived a very easy life in the palace, so now he tried to live the opposite way, with little to eat, rags to wear, no home, and no possessions. But eating only one grain of rice a day, his body became very thin, and he felt if he continued in this way, he would die before he had a chance to really live. Sitting on the edge of a field, alone, he thought, "There must be another way."

At that moment, a young girl came across the field, bringing him a bowl of rice porridge. And she said simply, "This is for you." He smiled, thanked her, and, grateful, ate the nourishing food.

He left his friends behind, stood at the foot of a great spreading fig tree, and said, "I will not move from this spot until I attain enlightenment, until I wake up to the truth of life." He settled cross-legged under the tree, and soon a crafty creature called Mara saw him sitting there. "What right has that young man got to sit there, so still, as if he were better than me?"

Mara sent all kinds of distractions to get Siddhartha to move. First Mara sent beautiful women, who tried to tempt him to dance. Siddhartha sat still. Then Mara sent servants bearing trays heavy with delicious-smelling food. Siddhartha sat still. Then Mara called on an army that came from the sky, shooting arrows toward the young man sitting under the tree. Siddhartha sat still. As his kind eyes looked up at the sky, the arrows became flowers, dropping gently from the sky like an early snow. And Siddhartha sat still.

Finally, the young man touched the ground with one hand and lifted the other toward the sky. The earth trembled with his courage and strength. He looked up and saw the morning star, and suddenly he understood who he was and what he had been born to do. We can't be sure exactly what happened there that morning. Perhaps Siddhartha understood that fear and sorrow, suffering and sadness, come and go but that there is also great peace and joy when we find our place in this wondrous universe. He wanted to share his awakening with others. He rose and went to find his friends, and from that day on, he met with and taught whoever wanted to learn the great truths of this world.

LET'S TALK ABOUT IT

Why do you think Siddhartha needed to leave home? What happened when he ate very little food for a long time? The fig tree that the Buddha sat under came to be called the Bodhi tree, or the tree of awakening; why did he decide to go and teach other people about what he discovered under the Bodhi tree?

❧ PRACTICES ❧

PEACE BELL

It's nice to have a bell in your house that you can ring now and then when you want to have a moment of peaceful quiet. I had a bell like this in my classroom to ring when we wanted a moment of peace, and my third-graders called it the "Peace Bell." I hope an adult will help you find a bell like this if you don't have one already. Usually this kind of bell is shaped like a bowl and you hit it with a small wooden stick. Whenever someone in your family rings the bell, the sound will get everyone's attention. Then ring the bell a second time and, wherever you are in your house, just stop and take three deep breaths. See if you can listen to the sound of the bell until you can't hear it anymore. Notice how you feel afterward.

This activity, just stopping in the middle of your life for a moment, is a kind of meditation.

GASSHO

In Zen practice, when we are done sitting still, we put our palms together, with our fingers pressed together, in front of our heart. Then we bow slightly from the waist. This is called *gassho*. Once a boy asked me, "Why are you Zen people always bowing to each other?" I asked him, "Well, what do you think about that?" And he said, "Is it kind of like the Buddha in me is bowing to the Buddha in you?" (That was a moment of Zen!)

SITTING ZAZEN

Set your timer for five minutes. Ring your peace bell three times and listen until you can't hear it anymore. Sit up straight in a chair, with your hands folded in your lap. Or sit cross-legged on the floor with your back straight. Imagine there is a thread lifting up through the top of your head. Close your eyes or just have them open a tiny bit. Take a few deep breaths and then let your breath come and go without trying. Just sit quietly for a few minutes and notice what your breath and your body feel like when you sit very still. Can you feel the air coming in and out of your nose? Can you feel your chest and tummy rising and falling as you breathe? Can you let your thoughts come and go without holding on to them? See if you can feel your whole body, all at once, from the top of your head to the bottoms of your feet. When your timer chimes, ring the bell one time to signal the end of zazen and then gassho.

HAIKU JOURNAL

At the end of each chapter of this book, you will find a haiku. This kind of short, three-line poem began in Japan, and you might have fun writing them yourself. The first line has five syllables, the second has seven syllables, and the third has five syllables. Haiku are often about nature and how we live in the world. In your journal, try writing a seventeen-syllable poem, or ask someone to help you write down your ideas. You might choose to write about clouds, the wind, the rain, the night sky. You can clap out the syllables of each line or count them on your fingers.

This haiku about zazen was written by Vedant Mishra, age ten:
How nice it is here, (*5 syllables*)
Sitting so still in the sun, (*7 syllables*)
And just observing. (*5 syllables*)

EVERYTHING IS CONNECTED

We know, because of science and our own hearts, that we are deeply connected to nature. As a child, Greta Thunberg, who was born in Sweden, became concerned about global climate change; she didn't feel that grown-ups were doing enough to protect the environment. Her efforts have inspired millions to take action. Greta says, "You are never too small to make a difference." In this story, a woman takes care of an injured bird and mysteriously finds a bright red cap that helps her hear the voices of animals and plants. She learns about how we are connected to the trees, and she teaches that wisdom to someone who needs it.

Story: The Cry of the Camphor Tree

There once was a woman who made her living gathering healing herbs in the forest to sell in the marketplace. She had learned from her grandmother exactly which plants were good for which ailments—and which plants to avoid. Before she set out in the morning for her daily work, she would sit quietly in a small temple near her hut.

One day, when she was sitting zazen in the temple, a bird, just learning to fly, came through the window and crashed into the temple wall. The woman picked him up and soothed him until he cocked his head, smiled at her, and flew back out the window. When the woman turned around, a bright red cap had appeared on the altar. When she put the cap on her head, she could suddenly hear the voices of the birds and even the whispers of the trees around the temple.

The next day she took her basket and wandered under the trees, looking for herbs. Suddenly she came to a grand house with a thatched roof. Two birds sat in a tree above, and the woman, wearing the bright red cap, could understand them talking to each other:

"How goes it in your neck of the woods?" said one of the birds. "Don't you live on the thatched roof of that house?"

"Yes," replied her friend, "but the master is not well. He cut down a camphor tree and built a teahouse on top of the stump. That poor tree keeps trying to grow but it can't. The wealthy man doesn't know that as long as the tree is ill, he will be ill too."

When she listened carefully, the woman could hear the camphor tree, moaning in pain underneath the teahouse. "Someone, please help me! I can't stretch my branches and leaves into the sky. As long as I am ill, the master will be ill, because our fates are tangled together like leafy vines!"

The woman knew that if she told this story to the man and his wife, they would think she was crazy, so she pretended to be a fortune-teller. "Fortunes told! Fortunes told!" she cried. Knocking at their door, she said to the wife, who answered the door, "I would be happy to tell you your fortune if you will offer me a bed for the night."

"Please come in! You are just in time! My husband isn't well, and nothing we have tried has helped him. Perhaps you can find out what's wrong."

"Did your husband have a teahouse built recently?" the woman asked.

"Why yes, how did you know?" The wife was surprised.

"Well, I'm a fortune-teller. I know all kinds of things! Let me sleep in the teahouse tonight, and I will tell you in the morning how to help your husband."

The next day, the woman and the man's wife sat down together with a pot of hot tea. "Your husband is sick because there is a camphor tree trying to grow under your teahouse. We can't live without trees. Trees give us oxygen and medicine and, if you carefully dig up the camphor stump and plant it where it can grow free, it will provide beautiful shade and its deep roots will keep your garden from washing away in the winter rains. When the tree is well, your husband will be well too."

The gardeners and the workers came and tore up the floor of the teahouse, removing the stump and planting it in a wide-open space, where it could send up healthy branches and leaves and where its roots could curl deep into the earth. The man quickly recovered. With the silver the "fortune-teller" received for her help, she was able to retire to her forest temple to meditate and, wearing her magic red cap, she could listen to and help the animals and the trees of the forest all the long days of her life.

Adapted from a Japanese folktale

LET'S TALK ABOUT IT

Do you ever wish you could hear what animals are saying to one another? What animals would you especially like to understand? Why does the woman in the story pretend to be a fortune-teller? Talk about all the things that trees give us . . . If you look around your house, you will find so many things that come from trees!

§ PRACTICES §

NATURE ZAZEN

Go out in your backyard or to a park. Sit quietly and see how much
you can hear when you really open your ears and listen carefully. Can
you hear the birds? Can you hear the wind ruffling the leaves of a tree?
Maybe you can even hear some busy insects. If you live in the city, you
need to listen to the sounds of nature that can be heard underneath the
traffic and the people! When we practice sitting quietly like this, even
when there is noise around us, we start to see that we can carry our own
peace inside of us.

A RICE CAKE

Hold a rice cake in your hand. What can you see in that rice cake?
Can you see the sun and rain that helped the rice grow? Can you see the
farmer who planted, tended, and harvested it? Can you see the person
who drove the bags of rice to the place where it was made into rice cakes
and packaged and then sent out to stores? Can you see the storekeeper's
mother and father and their mothers and fathers? Now, slowly eat the
rice cake, and it will become *you*! Make sure you take one small bite at
a time. Close your eyes and taste each bite completely. Now the rain
and sun and rice and the farmers are all a part of you, and you are part
of them!

BEING GRATEFUL FOR OUR FOOD

In Zen practice, before we eat our food, we say, "Innumerable labors
brought us this food. We should know how it comes to us." This means
that many plants and animals and people work together to feed the

whole world. Before you eat dinner with your family, appreciate the way the food looks on your plate. Take some time to talk about the beings—the plants, the animals, the people, the environment, the cook—that helped bring you the wonderful food that keeps you all alive. And thank them! In Zen practice, we gassho, or bow, before we eat to show this gratitude.

YOUR OWN SPECIAL PLANT

The man in the story learns that he needs to take care of the camphor tree in order to take care of himself. You can go to a plant nursery and buy a plant to take care of. The people who work at the nursery will help you pick out a plant that will grow well in your room or right outside your house or apartment. Find out what you need to do to take care of the plant. What is its name? How much water does it need? How much sunlight does it like? A grown-up can help you find the best spot for your plant. The plants in our homes give us beauty and oxygen—and taking care of them makes us feel good too!

NATURE HAIKU

Can you write a haiku in your journal about your connection to nature? Here's mine:

Looking at the stars,
I am part of them, and they
Are also in me.

EVERYTHING
CHANGES

Shunryu Suzuki Roshi helped bring Zen practice from Japan to the United States. He was the first teacher at San Francisco Zen Center. When someone asked him if he could explain Buddhism in just a few words, he said, "Everything changes." We can notice the truth of this if we just watch the seasons change, if we watch the weather change, if we see our younger sibling growing taller, if we notice that our moods and minds change many times a day. If we are going through a difficult time, at least we know that it won't last forever. If we are going through a great time, we know that this time won't last forever either! This is a famous story about a young boy and his Zen teacher.

Story: The Broken Teacup

Ikkyu was a clever boy who lived in Japan a very long time ago. He slept in a corner of the zendo—the meditation hall—in a temple in Kyoto, and his teacher was a very stern Zen master. The boy's job was to sweep the entrance to the temple in the morning and the evening and to make tea for his master and for the guests who came to visit the temple.

In Japan, tea ceremony is a special art, and Ikkyu's master had spent many years studying the art of tea. There was one teacup that he liked especially. It was a mysterious shade of blue, with the image of a graceful goldfish that looked like it was swimming in deep water.

One day, Ikkyu rose with the temple bells and swept the path as he did each day. While the monks were sitting zazen in the zendo, he built a small fire in the hearth to heat water for morning tea. He wanted to please his teacher, so he stood on a three-legged stool and reached up to a high shelf where the master kept his special goldfish teacup.

Uh-oh! The stool began to wobble and Ikkyu fell off, crashing to the floor. He jumped up and brushed himself off, unharmed. But the teacup, the very special teacup that his master loved so dearly, had broken into a dozen pieces. Ikkyu quickly picked up his broom, swept up the pieces, and wrapped them in a red cloth, tying the four corners together in a knot.

When zazen was over, and the bells' ringing and the monks' chanting had faded away, Ikkyu heard his master's footsteps coming toward him in the hallway. The mischievous boy hid the small red bundle behind his back.

When the master came into the room, Ikkyu was waiting for him. "Master," he asked innocently, tilting his small face up to his teacher, "why must people die?"

The master was fond of the boy, and his face broke into a patchwork of wrinkles as he smiled down at him. He laid a gentle hand on Ikkyu's head. "Because, my boy, that is the way things are. That is the way of life. Everything that is must someday come to an end."

"Master," said the boy, holding out the red bundle containing the broken teacup, "I'm sorry to say that it was time for your favorite teacup to come to an end."

The old master couldn't help it—he threw his head back and laughed out loud. "Let's have a cup of tea!" he said. And he took two teacups from the shelf.

Ikkyu grew up to be a poet, a flute player, and a Zen master. And he also became a master of the tea ceremony.

Adapted from an ancient Japanese tale

LET'S TALK ABOUT IT

Why does the boy tell the master, "It was time for your favorite teacup to come to an end"? And why does the master laugh when he says it?

§ PRACTICES §

GLITTER ZAZEN

You and a grown-up can create a "glitter jar" to help you when you have strong emotions. "Everything changes," including our feelings!

1. Find and clean a clear, empty twelve-ounce jar with a lid. A mayonnaise jar is perfect.
2. Fill the jar with water, leaving about an inch at the top.
3. Add some clear glue, replace the lid, and shake the bottle so the glue spreads through the water. The glue will make the glitter fall slowly.
4. Add a heaping teaspoon of big glitter sequins. They will fall slowly.
5. Add a heaping teaspoon of small glitter. This will fall more quickly.
6. Replace the lid and make sure that it is screwed on tight! This can be your own "feelings" jar. (My first glitter jar was given to me as a gift by my students Serina and Riyana. You can give one as a gift too!)
7. Ring your peace bell three times. Shake up the jar and put it down on a flat surface. Notice that the glitter swirls around and fills up the whole jar with its sparkling colors. As you watch, be aware of your breathing. You will see the glitter slowly settle on the bottom of the jar. This is like our strong emotions. We might be happy, angry, sad, uncomfortable, energetic, impatient, excited, or embarrassed. But in time, we can notice that our strong feelings begin to settle down and change. When you are ready, ring the bell one time and gassho.

SAND MANDALA

Once, a group of Tibetan monks came to our school to create a sand mandala. They worked on a large round table, using a special tool to create a beautiful circular design, one grain of painted sand at a time. After three days, we had a special ceremony, chanting as we enjoyed looking at the beautiful image. The students were very surprised when the monks carefully swept the sand image into a bag to be scattered in the garden. This represents the beauty and the impermanence of life. Impermanence means that everything changes, that nothing lasts forever. You can create a beautiful design on a sidewalk with chalk. Carefully create a colorful picture and make sure other people get a chance to look at and appreciate it. After three days, pour water over it and watch it change and disappear. Notice how you feel as your picture fades away. This also reminds us that when we are going through a difficult time, we know that it won't last forever!

HAVE A CUP OF TEA

Tea ceremony is a special practice to share with other people and to enjoy the making and drinking of tea. Invite a friend to have a cup of tea with you. Peppermint tea is very nice! You may need help from an adult to boil the water and pour it into the cups over the tea bags. A little honey is nice too. Sit quietly with your friend for a bit. Feel the warmth of the tea through the cup. Notice how the teacup looks and how the tea looks and smells. Blow on it a little bit before you take a sip and let the taste of tea fill up your mind and body. The tea you share with your friend becomes a part of both of you.

NATURE HAIKU: EVERYTHING CHANGES

Nature always shows us how everything changes. Can you write a haiku about the changes you see in nature? Here's one by Vedant Mishra:

The changing seasons:
Winter will go, spring will come,
But both will be back.

BEING KIND

His Holiness the 14th Dalai Lama, Tenzin Gyatso, is a Tibetan Buddhist leader who says, "My religion is kindness." We can always choose to be kind. We all want to be treated kindly, so why would someone want to be unkind? It's mysterious. Sometimes we just forget all about kindness and say things that we don't feel so good about. We let a friend down. We talk about a friend behind their back. We treat a brother or sister badly. The important thing is to notice how this makes us feel and try to do better next time. If we do hurt our friend or sibling, we can always try to make things right again. A kind word and an apology can go a long way. In this story, a woman spreads a rumor about her rabbi, the leader of her Jewish community, and then tries to make things right again.

Story: Feathers in the Wind

There once was a humble shop in the middle of a small village. It was nothing fancy, but the shopkeeper made sure that she had everything on the shelves that the people of the village might need: bags of flour, sugar, and tea; baskets full of apples, potatoes, and onions. If the shopkeeper didn't have it, you probably didn't need it.

One day, a woman entered the shop to buy a needle and thread. The shopkeeper was distracted, comforting her baby in a rocking chair at the front of the shop. The only other person in the shop was the village rabbi. The woman almost greeted him, but then she couldn't believe her eyes. The rabbi was picking things up off the shelves and putting them right into his pockets! An onion, an apple—they all disappeared into the big pockets in the rabbi's coat.

The woman forgot all about the needle and thread. She couldn't wait to tell her friends what she had seen.

"Our rabbi is a common thief!" she told her neighbor. "I saw him stealing from the shopkeeper while her back was turned!"

Well, that neighbor told another neighbor, and that neighbor told another neighbor until the whole village was buzzing with the news. Soon all the neighbors gathered around the village well and decided that the woman should go and tell the shopkeeper what she had seen in the shop that morning.

The woman stepped into the shop, and the shopkeeper cocked her head. "Can I help you?" she asked.

"I don't know how to say this, so I'll just come out with it. I saw the rabbi stealing from you this morning! He was taking things right off the shelf and putting them in his pockets!"

The shopkeeper put her hands on her hips, threw her head back, and laughed and laughed. "Why, silly woman, our rabbi is as honest as the day is long. I trust him so much that I let him take whatever he needs, whenever he needs it, and he pays me at the end of the month!"

The woman didn't know what to say, but she knew what she had to do. She went right to the rabbi's house and told him about her part in spreading the rumor about him.

"I am so terribly sorry. What can I do to make this right?" she asked.

The rabbi thought for a moment. "Go upstairs into the attic and open the window. There is an old pillow up there. Take these scissors and cut a hole in one end of the pillow and shake it out the window until all the feathers have flown away on the wind."

The woman thought this was very odd, but she did as she was told. As she shook the pillow out the window, the feathers caught the wind and were soon flying all over the place like the first snow of winter. She went back downstairs with the empty pillowcase.

"Well, Rabbi, I've done as you asked."

"Now," said the rabbi, "take that pillowcase and go outside and gather up all the feathers, wherever you can find them, and bring them back."

The woman was puzzled. "But, Rabbi, that's impossible. I could never find all of them."

"That's right," the rabbi said kindly. "Just as you can never call back all those feathers, you can never call back all the unkind and untrue words that have been spoken about me today in our village. Words spread easily, like feathers in the wind. Easy to let them go; not so easy to get them back. From now on, my good woman, think before you speak. Ask yourself, 'Is this kind? Is this true?'"

The woman had learned her lesson. And she told everyone she met that the rabbi was indeed an honest and forgiving man.

Adapted from a Hasidic folktale told by Rabbi Levi Yitzhak of Berdichev (1740–1809)

LET'S TALK ABOUT IT

How does the woman in the story feel when she realizes that she has been spreading news about the rabbi that isn't true? Why does the rabbi tell her to shake the pillow so the feathers go out of the window and away on the wind?

✿ PRACTICES ✿

HEART ZAZEN

Ring your peace bell three times and then just sit quietly for a few minutes listening to the bell until you can no longer hear it. Put two fingers on your heart and imagine you are breathing in and out of your heart for a few minutes. Imagine that your kindness is waking up and spreading from your heart out into the world. Ring your bell once, then gassho.

SPREADING KINDNESS

We all have special friends—people we like and feel comfortable with. But you might know someone you aren't such good friends with, someone who you don't usually play with. Maybe they seem different from you, and you aren't sure how to make friends with them. What would it feel like to be kind to that person? Don't make a big deal about it; just see if you can find a chance to talk to or play with someone you don't usually hang out with. You might even end up with a new friend!

LIVING KINDNESS JOURNAL

We can "live" kindness every day. The next time you treat someone kindly or help a friend who needs you, the next time you help set the table for dinner, the next time you take care of a pet, notice how it makes you feel inside. You can write about these things in your journal. One of my students said to me, "It's a lot more fun to be kind than it is to be mean!"

A SECRET GOOD DEED

Think of an act of kindness that you'd like to do for a friend or family member. See if you can do that good deed without "getting caught." You might tidy up a part of your house. You might give one of your toys to a sibling by wrapping it as a present and hiding it in their room for them to find. You could surprise your family by setting the table when they aren't looking or expecting it. We can feel good about doing kind things even if no one else knows about them!

KINDNESS HAIKU

Can you write a haiku about kindness? Here's mine:

Easy to be kind:
Just think about how you would
Want to be treated.

GENEROSITY

To be generous is to be willing to give something to someone else without expecting anything in return. We have many things to give to others. We can give them our time. We can give them our understanding. We can bake them a batch of cookies. Notice how good it feels when you are generous. Generosity is another way of noticing that we are all connected to one another. Sometimes we don't feel like being generous. Maybe it's because we think we won't have enough for ourselves. Maybe it's because we forget how good it feels to give something to someone else. In this story, a traveling monk teaches a whole village how good it feels to be generous with what we have.

Story: Stone Soup

There was once a traveling Monk who made his way through the world, seeing what there was to see and learning what there was to learn. He was such a gentle person that the animals of the forest would shyly come out of the underbrush to greet him, and birds perched on his shoulders. He wore a straw hat on his head, and he carried a begging bowl with him because he depended on the generosity of others in order to get food to live.

One fine spring day, tired and hungry, he took a path through the forest and soon found himself in a small village. He sat on a low stone wall near a rushing river as the villagers went back and forth. It had been a hard winter, and no one seemed very friendly.

The Monk's stomach growled with hunger as he held out his begging bowl to one villager after another. But they hurried past, silent, scowling, without a glance or a word—not for him and not for one another. "How can I help open their hearts?" the Monk thought to himself.

The Monk took a deep breath and began to build a small fire out of dried sticks and grass. He chose a large round stone from the bank of the river and washed it carefully with water. Soon a woman from the village came by and saw the Monk washing the stone. Overcome with curiosity, she asked the Monk, "Say, stranger, what are you up to?"

"Well," the Monk replied, "I'm going to make a batch of soup. Would you care to join me?"

The woman looked around. "But what kind of soup?"

The Monk laughed. "Why, stone soup, of course! I've chosen the best stone to be had but, silly me, I don't have a pot to cook it in!"

The villager laughed. "Why, you can't make soup out of a stone!"

"I know it sounds strange, but it's an old temple recipe. If you would be so kind as to lend me a large pot, I can get started. And, by the way, if you happen to have a carrot or two, that would make it even tastier!"

The villager hurried off and soon returned with a fine big pot. They filled the pot with water from the river and added the heavy round stone. The woman pulled out two carrots from her apron pocket. She cut them up with a knife she had on her belt and dropped them in. "Just so!" she said.

Soon word spread through the village and a small crowd gathered. All were curious to see if you really could make good soup out of a stone.

"I don't suppose anyone could spare a couple of potatoes. They really go well with stone soup," said the Monk. Magically, four potatoes found their way through the crowd.

"If anyone has an onion, we could add that to the soup too," someone said. A neighbor produced an onion from his pocket. Into the soup.

"I have some herbs!" said a man in a yellow cap. He offered basil and thyme and bay leaf to the boiling water. "I have some noodles!" cried his wife.

Now a delicious smell began to waft through the air, drawing more of the villagers to the bubbling pot. Beans and peas and corn found their way into the soup. Bowls and spoons appeared. The soup was ladled up and passed around. The villagers, who had been so silent and grim during the hard winter months, began to smile and laugh and chat with one another. They remembered their old friends and how good it felt to open their hearts and share a good meal around a crackling fire.

When the stars began to dot the black velvet of the night sky, the villagers began to shake hands, to hug one another, and to wish one another a good night's sleep, returning to their homes. The woman took the Monk's hands and said shyly, "If you need a place to lay your head, there is a soft pile of hay in my barn and a warm quilt waiting for you."

"Thank you for your generosity," said the Monk simply.

"It's true!" exclaimed a little girl, riding home on her father's shoulders. "You really can make a fine soup out of a stone. That is, if everyone helps!"

Adapted from a European folktale

LET'S TALK ABOUT IT

How does the Monk trick the people of the village? What do the villagers learn from the Monk's trick? The villagers enjoy eating the soup with one another. Can you think of something that is more fun to do with other people than it is to do by yourself?

§ PRACTICES §

SOUP ZAZEN

There is an old Chinese saying: "Many hands make much work light."
Ask some friends and an adult to help you make some soup. You can use
a favorite family recipe or look one up together. It might be fun to ask
each of your friends to bring one or two ingredients to cook so that you
are all contributing something, like the villagers in the story. You can
even put a clean stone into the soup, just for fun. It will be important for
an adult to supervise cutting vegetables and using the stove. Watch your
fingers!

SERVING YOUR SOUP

Set the table with a pretty cloth. Get help lighting some candles and
make a nice centerpiece of flowers or leaves. Making a pretty place to
enjoy food with friends and family is a kind of generosity. Ladle the
soup into bowls—make sure you set aside the stone if you used one!
You might want to have a nice crusty loaf of bread and some butter to
eat with your soup. Gassho to your friends and to the many beings that
made it possible for you to make and enjoy this soup.

SILENT EATING

Try this with your guests: Eat your food silently for a bit, tasting every
bite. Feel the sensations in your mouth as you taste everything. Enjoy
the feeling of it all entering your body and becoming part of you.

GENEROSITY JOURNAL

In your journal, write about a time when someone was generous with you and how that made you feel. Can you think of a time when you did something generous? How did that make you feel? Write about it!

GENEROSITY HAIKU

In your journal, write a haiku about your soup or about generosity. Here is Vedant's:

> When a penny is
> Given to someone else, it
> Becomes one hundred.

LEARNING
PATIENCE

Being patient means being able to go through difficulties without getting upset. Sometimes we feel so impatient that we feel like we could just "jump right out of our skin," as the saying goes. We jiggle our feet, tap our pencils, and wiggle around in our seats. Do you ever feel like that? It's natural to feel impatient sometimes, but if you want to be more comfortable, you can calm yourself down by taking some deep breaths and noticing where you are and what's around you. There is always something interesting to see! Being patient can also mean being gentle with other people and giving them a chance to just be who they are without trying to change or control them. In this story, a woman is unhappy and impatient with her family. She goes to her rabbi, a wise man and the leader of her Jewish community, to get some help. In the end, she learns how to be more patient with the people she loves.

Story: It All Depends

There was once a woman who lived in a tiny hut with her husband, their four children, and her elderly parents. It was hard enough being crowded together in the hut during the summer months, but in the winter, it was unbearable. The woman fought with her husband, her parents fought with each other, and the children tussled and wrestled and whined until the woman thought she might lose her mind.

The house shook with angry voices:

"You always . . . !"

"You never . . . !"

"It's MY turn!"

"No, it's MY turn!"

Everyone was irritable and impatient with one another. And they couldn't even go outside because it was so cold that their eyebrows froze, and their breath turned into clouds of ice in front of them. Finally, one cold night, the woman could take it no longer. She lost her temper and yelled at her family, *"Genug shoyn!* Enough already!"

The next morning, the woman pulled on a thick coat, shoved her freezing feet into her boots, and went to talk to her rabbi, who was known far and wide as the wisest of men. "Surely he can help," the woman grumbled to herself as she slogged through the deep snow.

She told her sad story to the rabbi, who sat in silence, stroking his long gray beard.

Finally, the rabbi cleared his throat and spoke: "You are indeed in an impossible situation. Tell me, do you have some chickens?"

"Why . . . yes, we have three chickens," the woman answered, wondering what chickens had to do with anything.

"Bring them into the hut," said the rabbi.

"If you say so, Rabbi," said the woman, her forehead wrinkled in confusion.

She went home and, even though everyone thought she was crazy, she brought the chickens into the hut. Now things were even worse. On top of all the usual noise and chaos, the chickens were squawking and flapping around; feathers floated everywhere, making everyone sneeze. The woman was even more impatient. She went back to the rabbi and told him how much worse things were.

"Yes, yes, I see what you mean," said the rabbi. "Tell me, do you have any goats?"

"Why . . . yes, we have two goats," the woman answered, wondering what goats had to do with anything.

"Bring them into the hut," said the rabbi.

With a deep sigh, the woman replied, "If you say so, Rabbi."

She trudged back home and, though everyone thought she was crazy, she brought the two smelly goats into the hut. Now things were much, much worse. The chickens squawked and crowed and flapped, the goats bleated and butted one another and the children, and the woman was even more impatient and irritable. She went back to the rabbi and told him that things were even worse than before.

"Yes, yes . . ." the rabbi said to the woman. "That sounds quite unpleasant. Tell me, do you happen to have a cow?"

The woman could see where this was going.

"If you say so, Rabbi," she said.

She went back home and, though everyone thought she was crazy, she brought the cow into the hut. Now the chickens were squawking and flapping, the goats were bleating and butting, and no one could think straight because of the loud moos of the uncomfortable cow. The next day, the woman returned to the rabbi.

"Dear Rabbi, your wisdom is known far and wide. I'm sure you know what's best, but I came to you with a problem and now things are much, much worse. What can I possibly do to make them better?"

"I'll tell you what," said the rabbi, "go back home and put all the animals back in their shed."

A big smile broke out on the woman's face. "If you say so, Rabbi!"

She went home and took the animals out of the hut. The woman and her family cleaned their home from top to bottom with buckets of warm, soapy water. Suddenly all was peaceful and quiet, with just the woman, her husband, their children, and her parents. They had room to move around, and they could sleep soundly at night without worrying about chickens landing on their heads or goats bleating in their ears.

The next day, the woman returned to the rabbi.

"Dear Rabbi," she said, "I don't know why your plan worked, but my life is so much better now. We are all getting along. We are all patient and calm, and our house is neat and clean and peaceful. I don't know how you did it!"

"Well," said the rabbi with a twinkle in his kind eyes, "I guess it all depends on how you look at things!"

Adapted from a Yiddish folktale

LET'S TALK ABOUT IT

Why does the rabbi have the woman bring the animals into the house? At the end of the story, the woman is right back where she started, so why is she so much happier? Why does the rabbi say, "It all depends on how you look at things?"

§ PRACTICES §

TREE ZAZEN

Trees are very patient. They just grow where they are and give back
beauty, stability, and shade. Go outside to a tree in your backyard or ask
a grown-up to take you to a park and find a nice tree there. Sit down on
the ground with your back to the tree. See if, as you breathe, you can
breathe in the patience of the tree as you sit quietly for a few minutes,
supported by the tree. You can make a beautiful rubbing of tree bark.
Take a crayon—or two or three—and peel off the paper wrapper. Place
a piece of white paper on top of the bark and, holding the crayon on its
side rather than with the tip, carefully rub the crayon back and forth
until the pattern of the bark comes through. You can experiment with
making a design of different colors. Gassho to thank the tree!

JUST BREATHING

The next time you are waiting in line for your turn at the swings or the
play structure, you might feel impatient. If you aren't talking with a
friend, try coming back to the feeling of your breath coming in and out
of your body. Can you feel the air coming in and out of your nose? Can
you feel your chest expanding a little as you take in a breath? Can you
feel the bottoms of your feet resting on the ground? See if you can have
the feeling that breath is filling up your whole body!

PLANTING SEEDS

You might have some seeds right in your house. Beans and lentils are
actually seeds. Popcorn is a kind of seed. There are seeds in apples,
oranges, and peaches. Peppercorns are seeds, and some of the other

spices we use for cooking, such as cardamom or cumin, can come in seed form. You can also get seeds in a package at a nursery. The people at a plant nursery can give you advice and help you find a "starting mix" of soil in which to sprout some seeds. (Garden soil isn't best for starting seeds because it is heavy and can have unhealthy things in it.) Put the starting mix in a clear plastic container. You can plant the seeds on the sides, in between the container and the starting mix, so you can watch them grow. Water the seeds so the mix is about as damp as a sponge. Make sure you keep the mix damp, but be careful not to flood it. But here's the thing: you will have to be patient because it might take a few weeks for the seeds to grow! Then you can carefully remove the sprouts in their starting mix and put them in a bigger pot or in the ground and cover them with a layer of soil—not too deep and not too shallow. Water them carefully, but don't overwater them. Waiting for seeds to grow takes patience, and it is a great mystery that they can actually sprout and grow into a new plant so much bigger than a seed! Even a giant redwood grows from just a tiny pod.

SPROUTING CARROTS

Take three or four nice-looking carrots and wash them. Then—and you might need help with this from an adult—cut them off at the wide end, not the pointy end, so that there is about an inch of carrot left on each top. Try to make the cuts straight across so the carrot tops can sit flat. Make sure you leave the nubs where the leaves grew out of the tops. You can eat the other part of the carrots: use a vegetable peeler to peel off the skin from the long part that is left and eat them or share them with a friend. Take the top parts of the carrots that you have cut off and set them in a shallow bowl or jar lid of water with the cut parts down. Don't cover them completely; just put a little water to cover this part of the carrots about halfway up. The water will evaporate a bit each day so you will need to keep an eye out and add a little more water when needed.

I won't tell you what is going to happen, but if you wait patiently, something beautiful will happen to your carrot tops.

PATIENCE HAIKU

In your journal, write a haiku about being patient or enjoying this moment. Here's mine:

> Taking a deep breath,
> I know I am here right now,
> Living this moment.

WHOLEHEARTED EFFORT

Sometimes we think we aren't good at something. We might not realize that if we keep trying, if we keep practicing, we can get better at almost anything we try. Michael Jordan, the famous basketball player, said, "I've missed more than 9,000 shots in my career. I've lost almost 300 games. Twenty-six times I've been trusted to take the game-winning shot and missed. I've failed over and over and over again in my life. That is why I succeed." I think Michael is saying that he is able to succeed because he keeps on trying. That is called "wholehearted effort." This is my version of a well-known story about a tortoise and a hare who have a race. Hare's boasting and bragging don't win the race—it's Tortoise and her wholehearted effort.

Story: The Tortoise and the Hare

Once, long ago, some animals of the forest came together in the shade of a glorious chestnut tree for an afternoon visit. As the animals chatted with one another, Hare's boasting voice could be heard above all the others.

"My ears are longer than any of *yours!*" he bragged. "And my legs are longer and stronger too. Not one of you has fur like mine! My fur is brown in the summer and white in the winter so that I can hide from my enemies. And let's face it, no one can run faster than I can! In fact, I will challenge any of you to a race!"

Squirrel was silent. Earthworm curled up in a little ball. Badger looked away.

"I thought so! You are all afraid. Will not one of you take me up on my dare?"

Suddenly a solitary voice was heard. "I'll try."

"What's that? Who's that?" cried Hare.

"Why, it's me, Hare, your old friend Tortoise."

At this, all the animals laughed long and hard. The idea of Tortoise racing Hare was just too funny. Beaver held his sides and rolled on the ground. Up in the branches of the chestnut tree, Sparrow chuckled with glee.

"That's a good one!" said Hare. "No, I'm serious. Will anyone race me?"

"Well, I'm serious too," replied Tortoise.

Hare looked around, winking at the other animals. This was his idea of fun!

"How about right now?" he asked Tortoise.

"Fine by me," Tortoise said. "Badger, would you draw a starting line in the dirt, and Sparrow, do you see that large boulder way off in the distance? Fly over there and peck a finish line for us."

All the animals gathered at the starting line to watch the race.

In her tiny voice, Field Mouse cried, "On your mark, get set, go!"

Hare took off in a blur. Tortoise put one foot in front of the other and started her long journey.

After a little while, Hare looked back and saw that Tortoise had barely begun. He threw his head back and laughed out loud. Showing off, he decided to lie down under a tree and pretend to go to sleep. He would watch Tortoise out of his half-closed eyes and when she got close, he would leap up and embarrass her by racing to the finish line. There was only one problem: Hare was soon fast asleep—for real!

Tortoise, on the other hand, just kept putting one foot in front of the other, steadfast and true, moving tirelessly onward.

All the animals cheered when Tortoise crossed the finish line. They all trotted to join her there, picked her up, and carried her on their shoulders, laughing and congratulating her. She had proved that wholehearted effort could win the race, if she just put one foot in front of the other and kept trying!

Hare woke up when he heard all the cheering and he scurried away, embarrassed.

Adapted from Aesop's Fables

LET'S TALK ABOUT IT

To admire someone means to be able to appreciate something special about them. What do you admire about Tortoise? The other animals make fun of Tortoise, but she tries her best anyway. Has that ever happened to you? Why does Tortoise win the race? And why is Hare embarrassed?

❀ PRACTICES ❀

WHOLEHEARTED-EFFORT ZAZEN

If you have an important event in your life, like a test at school, a sporting event, or a music or dance recital, or even a game on the playground, find a few moments before you begin to take a few deep breaths. No one even needs to know that you are doing this! Breathing—feeling your whole body, awake and aware—will help you gather your energy and your attention in order to make your best effort.

"IN EFFORT THERE IS JOY"

The Spanish artist Esteban Vicente said, "In effort there is joy." Talk to a grown-up—a parent or guardian, an aunt or uncle, a grandparent or a teacher—about their own effort to achieve something important. What did they want to be able to do, and what did they have to do to achieve it? Talk about what you both think that Esteban Vicente meant when he said, "In effort there is joy."

"JUST KEEP TRYING" JOURNAL

In your journal, write about a time when you didn't feel you were good at something but you kept trying. You might have learned to bake cookies or juggle or ride a bike or shoot a basket or learn your times tables or embroider cloth with a needle and thread or knit. Write about how it made you feel to have to try again and again before you learned how to do it. Were you discouraged? Did you give up and come back to it? How did it feel when you finally had a new skill? Do you think you could teach it to a friend or family member? You could also ask an adult to write down your thoughts for you, if you need help.

FAMILY HISTORY JOURNAL

Talk to a grown-up about someone in their family whom they admire. Every person we look up to has had to overcome great challenges to achieve their dreams. Perhaps a grandparent came here alone from another country. There may be a woman in your family who had to work especially hard because of how women were treated when she was growing up. Someone in your family might have had a disability that required special effort. They may have had to deal with poverty or prejudice. In your journal, write the person's name and why you admire them. Write down three obstacles or challenges that they had to fight against to realize their dreams. If that person is still alive, it will make their day if you write them a letter and tell them why you are thinking of them and why you admire them!

WHOLEHEARTED HAIKU

Bodhidharma is a famous figure in Buddhism. He is said to have brought Zen to China from India hundreds of years ago. There is a story that he sat still for nine years until his arms and legs fell off! (Do you think that could really happen?) You might have seen a small Daruma doll, with Bodhidharma's face and a weighted, rounded bottom. When you push him over, he bounces back up! This doll is a symbol of good luck and perseverance—which means "to keep trying, no matter what." The saying "Seven times down, eight times up" is about Bodhidharma's perseverance, because he keeps on trying. Can you write a haiku about wholehearted effort, about never giving up? Here is mine:

Seven times down and

Eight times up. Keep trying and

The path will open.

TAKING CARE OF THINGS

An important part of Zen is learning how to take care of things. The things we use every day take good care of us, and we should take good care of them. A good cook takes care of his knives because he couldn't prepare good food without their help. A good carpenter takes care of her tools because she couldn't build things without their help. Cooks and carpenters keep their knives and tools clean, and they put them back in the same place each time they use them so that they are there when they need them again. There is a saying in Zen, "Chop wood, carry water," which means "Every day, pay attention to what you are doing, and take care of things." In this story, a young monk enters the temple because he wants to see what Zen is all about.

Story: Wash Your Bowl

There was a young man who longed to enter the monastery so that he could practice Zen. He had heard tales of the great Zen masters and he wanted to be just like them, to be able to sit still with a calm mind and to grow in his knowledge and compassion.

He set off with just the clothes on his back and made his way up into the high mountains. The crooked path led him to a Zen temple, and he sat outside for three days, facing a wall, hoping that the master would notice him and let him in.

On the evening of the third day, Master Joshu silently slid open the wooden door of the temple and invited the young man to enter. It happened to be time for the evening meal, so the young man slipped off his shoes and put them neatly on the shoe rack, entered the zendo, sat down, and silently ate a bowl of rice porridge with the other monks.

When he was done, he approached the master and said, "I've just entered the monastery. Will you teach me?"

Joshu answered, "Have you eaten your rice porridge?"

The young monk answered, "Yes, Master, I have eaten."

Joshu said, "Then you had better wash your bowl."

At that moment, the young monk was enlightened—he understood something that can't be said in words.

Adapted from *The Gateless Gate* by Mu-mon

LET'S TALK ABOUT IT

Why does the young monk want to enter the monastery? Why do you think Joshu has him sit outside for three days before he invites him into the monastery?

❧ PRACTICES ❧

LETTING-GO ZAZEN

It is easier to take care of things if you don't have a lot of extra stuff that you don't need or use. First, think about your clothes, shoes, and toys and see if there are things that you don't need anymore. See if you are holding on to toys that you have outgrown. Other children can use them if they are still in good condition. Put those things aside to take to the Goodwill or the Salvation Army or pass them on to a friend or younger sibling. Check with a grown-up who can help you decide if it's really time to pass those things on and where to take them. (I still have my teddy bear, Teddy, from when I was little. There may be things you want to keep forever, even if they are worn and old, because they are like good friends.)

A PLACE FOR EVERYTHING

Decide the best place to keep the things you use. It makes sense to keep books on a shelf. Maybe you need containers for action figures or other toys. You will feel good if you know right where your art supplies are when you need them. What drawer do you want to keep your T-shirts in? Where do you put your dirty clothes?

MAKE YOUR BED

If you haven't learned how to make your own bed yet, ask a grown-up to show you how. Pull back the covers and then pull up the sheet and smooth it out and tuck it in. Then pull up the blankets or the comforter and smooth them out too. Fluff up your pillow. You can put it at the head of the bed or pull a bedspread over it. There is a great feeling in making your own bed when you get up every day, and it makes you feel that you are starting the day off by taking care of things.

BRUSH YOUR TEETH AND WASH YOUR FACE AND HANDS

If you take care of your teeth, they can last your whole life! Make sure that you know the best way to brush your teeth, and you can also learn how to floss your teeth. When you go to the dentist, the hygienist will show you how and might also give you a new toothbrush and floss . . . kind of like party favors! Washing your face and hands is another way to feel that you are starting out fresh each day.

EVERYDAY THINGS JOURNAL

Look around your room and pick up an object that you see or use every day. It could be a toy, a crayon, a paintbrush. Put it on a table and really look at it. What color is it? How does it rest on the table? Does it have a shadow? Are there reflections on the surface? Are there signs of wear and tear? Think about where you got it and how long you have had it. How do you feel about it? Do you like it? Dislike it? Now, take out your journal and a pencil. Turn to the next blank page in your journal and draw your object. Sketch very lightly with your pencil. Keep looking back at the object so that you can draw what it really looks like instead of what you *think* it looks like. Try not to erase anything you think is a "mistake." This is a way to really see and appreciate something that you see every day that you might not even notice. When you are looking at it, this everyday thing is actually inside your mind and body.

HELPING OTHERS

You can get a good feeling from helping others, and it makes them feel good too. Do you have some jobs that you do for your family? Ask a parent how you can help take care of things around the house. You are a part of your household, and you can help take care of it. Feeding a pet, setting and clearing the table, emptying the trash, helping to do the dishes, taking care of your own room, sweeping the floor: these are important jobs that need to be done around the house. You will enjoy doing these jobs if you pay attention when you do them and do them well, rather than rushing through to get them over with!

TAKING CARE OF THINGS HAIKU

Think about something specific that you want to take care of and write a haiku about it in your journal. Here is my haiku about taking care of things:

> When washing a plate,
> I hold it gently, as if
> Washing a baby.

WISDOM

Wisdom is made up of bravery and gentleness. Malala Yousafzai is a young Pakistani activist who fights for girls to be able to get an education. She said, "One child, one teacher, one book, one pen can change the world. . . . When the whole world is silent, one voice becomes powerful." We must be brave enough to stand up for ourselves and for others. But we can also be gentle enough to be kind to others and maybe even to forgive those who have hurt our feelings. This is a story about a gentle prince who learns how to defend himself as he finds within himself bravery, resilience, and the ability to forgive. At the end, you will learn about his secret weapon!

Story: Brave and Gentle

Long ago, in another place and time, there lived a King and Queen who longed to have a child. And it came to pass that one fine spring day, the Queen gave birth to a healthy son. On the day that he was to be named, a great celebration was held. The Queen asked the local fortune-tellers what the future held for the young prince.

One of them bowed and said, "He will be a wise and just king, following in his father's footsteps." Another said, "He will always keep the people in his heart and do what is best for them." And another said, "He will be a brave warrior, skilled in the use of five weapons."

Because of this last prediction, the King and Queen named their son Prince Five Weapons.

As a young boy, the Prince loved to sit under the Bodhi tree on the palace grounds and listen to the wind in the trees and watch the leaves shimmering in the sun. He loved to play with the children of the servants, and he was kind to everyone and to every plant and animal. If he saw a ladybug crossing his path, he would pick it up and move it out of danger.

The King and Queen loved their son but, because of his gentle ways, they began to wonder if he could grow up to be a great leader and a brave warrior. When the Prince was sixteen years old, the King gave him a leather pouch filled with gold coins so that he could travel to a distant city to study with a teacher who was known far and wide for her wisdom and skill. There, the Prince learned the history of his kingdom and the deep truths of mathematics and language. He was also taught to be an expert in the use of the five weapons that had given him his name.

When the Prince had completed his studies, his teacher presented him with the five weapons in which he excelled. "These will protect you as you travel back home. But the greatest gift you have is deep within you." And before Prince Five Weapons could ask her what she meant, his teacher quietly slipped inside her humble hut, and the Prince started off for home.

He soon came to a dense forest. Some travelers sat on the grass. As he started to enter the deep woods, one of the travelers cried out, "Turn around and go the other way! This path leads to the lair of a terrible Ogre. Anyone who meets him never returns!"

Prince Five Weapons drew himself up to his full height. Everything his teacher had taught him rose up inside of him, and he said, "I have no fear! Let me pass!"

"Suit yourself!" the traveler answered. "But don't say we didn't warn you!"

The Prince walked straight ahead, deep into the forest, filled with both excitement and dread. Was this Ogre just a myth? Would he encounter this monster and, if he did, would he survive?

Suddenly an enormous creature leaped out to block the path in front of Prince Five Weapons. So this was the Ogre! He was as tall as a tree, with a huge belly and shaggy fur that covered him from the top of his head to the tips of his toes. On his hands and feet were claws like razors and his eyes smoldered, red as fire. He opened his huge mouth and showed his sharp teeth and his long red tongue.

"Halt!" cried the Ogre. "And say goodbye to your life, for here it ends!" And he staggered with crashing footsteps toward the Prince, with smoke coming out of his eyes, his ears, and his mouth.

Prince Five Weapons was afraid, but he had his five weapons, and he knew what to do. "Don't come one step farther! If you mean to destroy me, I will defend myself with silver arrows!" he shouted.

The first two weapons given to him by his teacher were a bow and ten silver arrows. With one motion, he pulled a silver arrow out of his quiver, fitted it into his bow, and shot. But though he shot arrow after arrow, they just bounced off the Ogre and fell to the ground.

The third weapon was the spear. He aimed it at the Ogre's great belly and heaved it with all his might, but the spear also dropped harmlessly to the ground.

The fourth weapon was the club. He grabbed it and ran toward the Ogre, but when he swung the club at the Ogre's chest, it just got stuck in his thick, matted fur.

The Prince's own body was the fifth weapon. Though the Ogre howled and spit fire, Prince Five Weapons stood his ground.

"I still have another powerful weapon!" he shouted. "My fists!"

And with that, he pounded on the Ogre's massive chest with his fists, but the Prince's hands stuck tight to the shaggy fur. He wasn't ready to give up, so he kicked the Ogre as hard as he could. His feet, too, became tangled in the Ogre's pelt. Now his whole body was stuck to the Ogre, and he hung there like a puppet dangling from strings.

The Prince had used all five weapons, but was he now helpless? Maybe not, because suddenly he understood the strange words his teacher had spoken to him when they parted. "The greatest gift you have," she had told him, "is deep within you."

"Now will you give up?" roared the Ogre.

"Never!" yelled the Prince. "I have something inside of me that you can never defeat!"

Now he had the Ogre's attention.

"What could he be talking about?" thought the Ogre. "Maybe he is telling the truth! That would explain his crazy bravery and confidence! This could be the end of me . . ."

"With what other weapon do you challenge me?" he cried.

Prince Five Weapons replied, "I have a diamond-sharp sword within me, a sword far more powerful than your sharp claws and your teeth! If you want to find out about it, go ahead and eat me!"

He didn't say so, but he was speaking of the sword of wisdom and knowledge that had formed in his heart during his years of training with his teacher.

Somehow, to his own surprise, the Ogre believed him. He gently released Prince Five Weapons, prying the Prince's hands and feet from his ragged fur and lowering him to the ground.

"I bow to your greater strength," the Ogre said. "Now be on your way. You are free to go." His great head hung down.

But the Prince hesitated. He thought of the ladybugs and crickets he had saved from harm when he was little. Shouldn't he try to help this strange creature and save him from his own miserable ways?

"Ogre, you can change your life. You will never be happy as long as you bully and harm others—you will always live in a kind of dark loneliness. There is another way: Stop killing, stop lying, stop stealing, stop being cruel, and stop poisoning your own mind and body. If you do, you too will have access to a marvelous power."

He stayed for a while with the Ogre, teaching him the ways of gentleness. Together, they sat at the foot of a tall tree, sharing the joy of just being alive. The animals of the forest, who had lived in fear, shyly came to eat nuts and berries from their outstretched hands. The Prince put the Ogre in charge of making sure that all who came through this dark forest could travel safely.

Finally, as they parted, Prince Five Weapons told the Ogre his true secret: "The marvelous power I have is that I have learned to be my own best friend. If you can be a good friend to yourself, you are ready to be a good friend to others."

Adapted from an ancient Jataka tale from India

LET'S TALK ABOUT IT

The teacher of Prince Five Weapons tells him that his greatest gift is inside of him. He later understands what she meant. What is this gift? At the end of the story, why does the Prince decide to stay and spend time with the Ogre?

❦ PRACTICES ❦

BRAVERY ZAZEN

Ring your peace bell three times and sit in your zazen posture. When we sit up straight, with strength lifting us up through our spine and our shoulders rolled back, we are demonstrating our own strength and purpose. Feel the strength and bravery in your own heart. Sit like this for a few minutes, as still and powerful as a tall mountain. Then ring your bell and gassho.

RESILIENCE AND COMPASSION

In my third-grade classroom, I always had a sign on the wall that said "How can I find resilience within myself?" and "How can I show compassion to others?" *Resilience* is a wonderful word. It means being able to keep going and feel good about yourself even when things aren't going great. One of my third-graders came running over to me after he missed a shot in a basketball game and said, "I found resilience within myself!" *Compassion* means being able to feel what other people feel. If a friend falls down, you help them get up. If someone is being mean to someone else, you stand up for that person. Think of times when you found resilience within yourself and when you showed compassion to someone else. Thinking about this will help you do it again next time!

BRAVE AND GENTLE JOURNAL

In your journal, write about a time you were brave, or tell a helper about it and ask them to write it down for you. Give details and include any conversation you can remember. I bet your helper can tell you a story about being brave too. The Prince is kind to the Ogre, his former enemy.

Write about a time when someone was kind to you when you really needed some gentleness!

BIOGRAPHIES

It helps us find our own bravery if we read about real people who are brave. At the library or bookstore, find biographies of brave people. A biography or autobiography is the true story of someone's life. Jackie Robinson was the first African American baseball player to play in the major league. Because of his bravery and gentleness, he opened the door for other players who came after him. He said, "There's not an American in this country free until all of us are free." Who would you like to learn about? The children's librarian at your branch library will show you where to find biographies. You can take turns reading the books out loud with a grown-up and talk about them as you go along.

COMMEMORATIVE PLATES

After you have read some biographies of brave and compassionate people, you can create art to honor them. Get a plain white paper plate. Print the name of a special person on the top edge. On the bottom edge, write why they are famous. Draw and color a portrait of them on the flat part of the plate with markers or colored pencils. You can also make a colorful border around the edge. You might have a parent or grandparent who has been especially brave. Make a beautiful plate for them with their name on it and a portrait of them and give it to them.

SPECIAL PEOPLE HAIKU

Maybe by reading about brave and gentle people you will be inspired to write a haiku about one of them. Here is mine:

Jackie Robinson:
Both brave and gentle, he changed
The world forever.

FRIENDSHIP

When Buddha's companion Ananda asked him about the importance of friendship, the Buddha answered, "Friendship is everything, the whole of the holy life." The friends we choose and the friends who choose us are very important. They can add to our peace and happiness and our feeling that we belong to the world—or sweep those things away with an unkind word or a thoughtless action. A good friend brings out the best in us, and we feel good when we are around them. Sometimes we have conflicts or disagreements with our friends, and we might even forget how important they are to us. In this story, I have reimagined an ancient tale from India. See how Lion and Tiger remember that they can still be friends—even if they disagree with each other!

Story: Golden Sun, Silver Moon

Long ago, a lion and a tiger lived near each other in the forest. Now, you might think it strange that these two fierce beasts could be good friends.

But when they were very young, Tiger's mother had died, so Lion's mother took the tiny helpless tiger cub by the scruff of the neck and raised her as her own. Lion and Tiger grew up as brother and sister, playing tag, frolicking and tumbling in the long grass, and never noticing that one of them had stripes and one of them didn't and that only one of them had a fluffy mane.

One evening, when dusk began to creep over the sky, the two friends made their way to the crest of a hill and lay down together to watch the brilliant colors of the sunset floating on the calm water of the river. As the sun began to set, they noticed the full moon rising over the distant mountains.

"Tell me, Tiger," said Lion, "which do you think is more important, the sun or the moon?"

Tiger thought for a moment. She loved to hunt at night, and she would surely miss the good company of the full moon. But she had a feeling that the world would be a bleak and chilly place without the sun. "I think the sun is more important. What about you?"

"Well," said Lion, "I think the moon is more important. The sun is out during the daytime when it's light anyway, but it's dark at night. It would be even darker if not for the light of the full moon. Therefore, it's obvious that the moon is more important."

Tiger barked a rough laugh. "My friend, that doesn't make any sense. It's light during the day because the sun is shining. Nothing could grow or even survive without the sun. Therefore, the sun is more important."

"But, Tiger, you like to hunt at night. You would be stumbling around in the bushes and bumping into trees without the moon."

"Lion, if you put your brains in a bird, it would fly backward! The moon only glows because the sun is shining on it from a place we cannot see! Therefore, the *sun* is more important. I don't know if I can be friends with someone who can't even think straight!" Tiger was pacing around and shaking her head.

Lion had never thought about the sun and moon that way, but he was too embarrassed to admit it. So he stubbornly said, "Tiger, I don't know if *I* can be friends with someone who puts me down the way you do! Maybe it's best if we go our separate ways!"

Just then, they heard Owl in a tree up above. "What's going on down there? I'm trying to take a nap!" Owl needed to rest up before her nighttime hunting began.

"We're having an argument," said Tiger.

"Wait a minute, haven't you two been friends for a very long while?" asked Owl.

"We've been friends since we had tiny paws and baby teeth!" said Lion. "But we can't be friends anymore. This is the end!"

"What are you fighting about?" asked Owl.

"I say the moon is more important, and she says the sun is more important!" answered Lion.

Owl fluttered down to a lower branch. "You've been friends your whole lives long and you're going to end it over such a silly disagreement?"

Tiger and Lion looked at each other and then said together, "Can you help us solve this question?"

The wise owl, who would one day be reborn as the Buddha, thought for a moment. "Listen to me now," she said finally. "Sun and moon are friends. The golden sun lights up the day, and the silver moon lights up the night. And you light up each other's lives with your friendship. Now be on your way and let me get some sleep!"

From that day on, Lion and Tiger understood that they could disagree and still be friends.

Adapted from an ancient Jataka tale from India

LET'S TALK ABOUT IT

How did Lion and Tiger get to be friends? What are they fighting about? How does Owl help them? Do you think you can disagree with someone and still be friends?

§ PRACTICES §

FRIENDSHIP ZAZEN

Set your timer for five minutes and ring your peace bell three times. Take three deep breaths. Bring into your mind a person whose friendship is important to you. Picture them. What is it about them that you appreciate the most? What good memories do you have about your friend? What do you feel you need to do to be a good friend? Imagine that you are sending kindness and good feelings to your friend with each of your breaths. If you wish, you might want to bring other friends or family members to mind and send them kind thoughts.

THE PEACE PROCESS

A Zen Buddhist sangha is a group of people who live together or close to one another and practice Zen Buddhism, sitting zazen together in the zendo, or meditation hall, and working with one another. Together they cook and clean the temple and study the Buddha's teachings. But sometimes they don't get along so well with one another. Then they can use something called "conflict resolution" to mend their friendships. This way of healing friendships is very much like the Peace Process, a method that many teachers use with kids who disagree,

The Peace Process is a way to solve a problem with a friend or to help friends who are having a disagreement. You can try this yourself the next time you and your friends or your family members are having difficulty with one another, or you could help two people go through the Peace Process:

* First, one person shares how they feel without being interrupted. (It's best to talk about how the situation makes you feel rather than complaining about the other person. For example, "I feel angry and sad when you make fun of me.")
* Then the other person repeats, in their own words, what that person said. You can say, "Did they get that right? Is that close to what you said?"
* Now the second person shares how they feel without being interrupted.
* Then the first person repeats, in their own words, what that person said. You can say, "Is that right? Is that close to what you said and how you feel?"
* The first person shares what they need from their friend or family member going forward.
* The second person repeats what that person needs.
* The second person shares what they need from their friend or family member going forward.
* The other person repeats what that person says they need.
* See if both people can agree to what their friend or family member needs in the future to mend the hurt.
* If they can do it sincerely, they can hug or shake hands. And, in closing, encourage each of them to say something that they appreciate about one another.

FRIEND HAIKU

Our friends are so precious. Write a haiku about a particular friend or about friendship. This is mine:

What is more precious
Than a friend who will be there,
Even in the dark?

THIS PRESENT MOMENT

You have probably never been chased by a tiger. But have you ever been so worried that your worry was like a fearsome tiger that was chasing you? Have you ever felt so sad that the feeling of sadness filled your whole mind and body? Have you ever been so frightened that all you could imagine was some terrible thing happening? If we can turn toward the present moment, our worry or fear or sadness can melt away. Even when things are difficult, we can always find some sweetness and joy if we look for them. Take a nice deep breath before you read this story.

Story: Imagine!

Imagine you are hunting for mushrooms in the woods.

Fortunately, you find a big cluster of them at the foot of a big tree and begin to gather them and put them in a basket.

Unfortunately, when you look up, you see a tiger stalking you through the dark shadows of the forest.

Fortunately, you see the tiger in time. You drop the basket and run away. You are a fast runner, so you dodge the trees and soon come to an open meadow. You run as fast as you can, glancing back over your shoulder at the advancing tiger.

Unfortunately, you suddenly came to the edge of a steep cliff.

Fortunately, you don't fall off the edge.

Unfortunately, when you peer over the side, you see another big tiger pacing below. The tiger behind you is catching up with you and getting closer and, below, the other tiger is looking up at you and licking his lips, as his tail swishes back and forth, back and forth.

Fortunately, you are able to grab a vine and swing down out of reach of the tiger above and the tiger below.

Unfortunately, a white mouse and a black mouse creep out of a hole in the cliff and begin to chew on the vine at the same time.

Fortunately, you spot a juicy red strawberry nearby. With one hand, you pluck the strawberry and pop it into your mouth.

How very sweet it tastes!

Question: What do you do next? (The answer is below.)

Adapted from a story told by the Buddha

Answer: Stop imagining!

At the end of the story, why do you think the strawberry tastes so good? Why does the story tell you to stop imagining? Have you ever been really worried about something that didn't end up happening?

§ PRACTICES §

STRAWBERRY ZAZEN

Ring your bell three times. Take a strawberry and put it in your mouth.
Close your eyes and focus completely on the taste of the strawberry as
you chew. Strawberries aren't always available, so if you can't find one, a
raisin or another piece of fruit will also work for this activity. Sit quietly
for a few minutes, enjoying the taste in your whole body, then ring your
bell once and gassho.

WORRY JOURNAL

The next time you are worried about something, write about it in your
journal. What do you think is going to happen? How does your body
feel when you are worried? What can you do about it right now? Later,
be sure to notice how things actually turned out. A lot of the things we
worry about never actually happen—or they happen a lot differently
than we imagined. Doing this will help you the next time you are
worried!

COMPLETE RELAXATION

Sometimes our mind is so busy or so worried that it is hard to go to
sleep. Practice complete relaxation using these words. You might try this
at night in bed. It helps to have a parent, a guardian, a grandparent, or
an older sibling read these directions to you in a soft, slow voice:

* Take off your shoes and socks and lie down on your back on a rug or
  on your bed. If you are ready for bed, you can do this in your pj's.
  From inside your mind, look around your body and see how you feel.

* Take a few deep breaths and let your body feel heavy and relaxed.
* Scrunch up your face, stick out your tongue, wiggle your jaw. Now relax them.
* With your eyes closed, roll your head back and forth and then relax it.
* Make a fist with your right hand, tighten your whole arm, and lift it up a few inches. Gently let it go, roll your arm back and forth, and relax it.
* Do the same thing with your left hand.
* Now, point your right foot like a dancer, tightening your whole leg and lifting it up a couple of inches. Then gently drop your leg, roll it back and forth, and relax it.
* Do the same thing with your left leg.
* Now your body should feel quite heavy and relaxed. Feel your breathing coming in and out of your body and, with each breath, let your body sink down a little bit more. Feel the bed or floor where it touches your body.
* Now you are lying on the warm sand on a beach. You can hear the waves gently lapping at the shore. The wind is ruffling the palm trees. You feel your whole body, completely relaxed and free . . . Sweet dreams!

RELAXATION HAIKU

After you have tried the complete relaxation practice, see if you can write a haiku in your journal about how it feels. Here's mine:

Calm, in my body,
I ride the gentle wave of
This precious moment.

AFTERWORD

I hope that you and your family have had a good time reading these stories and trying some of these practices. Maybe you came across things that you weren't quite ready for or didn't want to try just yet. Maybe you will want to come back to them and do them another time—or even do some of them more than once. The Buddha said, "You must be a lamp unto yourself." This means, "Learn from your own experience and see what you find out along the way." Zen practice is something that takes a lifetime. After all, it's about our everyday life and how we live it. You will continue to learn new things and have new understandings, and I hope that you will always keep an open heart and an open mind toward new experiences and the many people who will come into your life. Be brave, be gentle, be kind, be generous, grow in wisdom, never give up, and worlds will open up for you. I wish you all the best on your journey . . . and maybe we will meet each other now and then along the path.

Why are we here?
We are here to see the beauty in the universe.
And to add to that beauty,
To be a light in the darkness.

—Wayne Harris

ACKNOWLEDGMENTS

Grateful thanks to Bala Kids for inviting me to do this project; to my dharma friends at Zen Center and at Lenox House; to the wonderful women of The Trees; to the friends and family who have always supported me; to my soul mates from The San Francisco School; to the many children I've taught who've taught me so much; to my beloved teacher, Eijun Linda Cutts; and to my daughter, Nova, who has always kept the welfare of children at the center of her heart. Special thanks to Ishaan, Vedant, Serina, and Riyana.

GLOSSARY

Aesop's Fables—Aesop's Fables come to us from a storyteller who lived in Greece hundreds of years ago. A lot of these stories are about animals, but they teach us how to be better people!

altar—An altar is a shelf or surface that is set aside as a special place. It can be covered with a pretty cloth and may include candles, incense, flowers, photographs of loved ones, and an image of the Buddha or other inspiring figures. It is a beautiful, peaceful place for your family to gather at special times.

begging bowl—Sometimes Buddhist monks carry bowls with them and the people passing by offer them food. The monks are thankful for whatever is given to them.

Bodhidharma—Bodhidharma was the Buddhist monk who is said to have brought Buddhism to China from India in the fifth or sixth century. The tippy Daruma doll is named after him—when you push it down, it bounces back up!

Buddha—Buddha means "an awakened person," and it usually refers to Siddhartha Gautama, who was born over twenty-five hundred years ago. His way of life and teachings are now called "Buddhism."

Buddha Hall—The Buddha Hall is a room in a Zen temple where the community meets to chant and perform services and ceremonies. This room has an altar, beautiful Buddhist figures, and grass mats called *tatami* to kneel on. It is a peaceful place to spend time with other people.

Buddhism—Buddhism is the way of life that is based on the teachings of Siddhartha Gautama: in life, there is suffering, and we can make that suffering a little easier by living with wisdom and compassion, trying to be kind and doing what we know is right.

camphor tree—The camphor is an East Asian tree that is in the laurel family. Camphor is a good medicine for infections. When you have a cold or cough, it feels good to rub a paste with camphor in it on your chest! This will help you breathe when you are stuffed up.

compassion—Compassion helps us feel what other people feel. We show compassion to others by listening to them, by spending time with them, and by being kind to them. We all need a little compassion!

Dalai Lama—The 14th Dalai Lama, Tenzin Gyatso, is the leader of the Tibetan people and is seen as a wise and kind teacher to the whole world. If you look for him on YouTube, you will see his smiling face, his warm laughter, and his wise words!

dharma—Buddha's teachings are called the "dharma"; *dharma* also means "the way things are."

enlightenment—In Buddhism, this is the word for awakening. The Buddha experienced an awakening to the truths of this life and taught those truths to others.

gassho—This is the Japanese word for bowing. Press your hands together in front of your heart with your fingers lined up and elbows slightly raised, and bow slightly from the waist. This can mean "thank you" or "hello" or "goodbye" or "I'm sorry" or "I see you and respect you."

generosity—When we are generous, we can give to others without expecting anything in return.

genug shoyn—This is a Yiddish expression for "Enough already!" You could say this to someone who is pestering you!

haiku—A haiku is a short form of Japanese poetry made up of seventeen syllables. A haiku has five syllables in the first line, seven syllables in the second line, and five syllables in the third line. These poems are often about nature and impermanence.

herbs—Herbs are green plants that can be used for medicine, tea, or flavoring food. You probably have some herbs, such as oregano and basil, in your kitchen!

Jataka tales—The Jataka tales are stories from India. It is said that the Buddha was born in the form of different animals before he was born as a human being and, finally, as the Buddha. The Jataka tales tell about these different lifetimes.

ogre—An ogre is a frightening monster. They don't exist in real life, but we can imagine them!

patience—To be patient means to be able to go through things that are difficult without getting upset. It takes a lot of patience to be a human being!

perseverance—When we persevere, we keep trying, no matter what.

practice—A practice is something that you do over and over again until it becomes part of your life. We can also practice performing an action to improve in that activity. Practice helps us meet the joys and challenges of life completely when they come our way.

rabbi—A rabbi, which means "teacher," is a spiritual leader in a Jewish community.

resilience—Resilience is the ability to bounce back, like a Daruma doll, from difficult situations. We show resilience when we don't let little disappointments get us down.

rumor—A rumor is a quickly spreading story that may not be true.

sadhu—The word *sadhu* comes from India. A sadhu is a person who has given up a lot of the comforts we take for granted and who seeks the truth behind everyday life.

sangha—A sangha is a community of people who come together to live according to the Buddha's teachings. Because we are all connected, we might say the whole universe is a sangha!

Shunryu Suzuki Roshi—Shunryu Suzuki Roshi was the Japanese priest who helped bring the practice of Zen Buddhism to the West in 1959. He founded the first Buddhist monastery outside of Japan, Tassajara Zen Mountain Center.

Siddhartha Gautama—Siddhartha Gautama is the name of the person known as the Buddha.

temple—A temple is a building where Buddhist monks live. They take care of the temple, and they meditate together, help others, and eat their meals there.

thatched roof—A thatched roof is a roof woven out of sticks and long grasses.

Three Treasures—The Three Treasures are Buddha, the teacher; Dharma, the teachings; and Sangha, the community.

vow—A vow is a promise that we make to ourselves and others about how we want to live.

wholehearted effort—Wholehearted effort is the intention to do our best even when things aren't going the way we want. Tortoise is slow, but she finally wins the race because of her wholehearted effort!

wisdom—Wisdom is knowing the right thing to do—and doing it! Wisdom can be a combination of bravery and gentleness. It also means knowing when to act and when not to act; when to speak and when not to speak. When we act with wisdom and take care of things and people, we even feel better about ourselves.

zafu—A zafu is a Japanese-style meditation cushion.

zazen—*Zazen*, which means "just sitting," is the Japanese word for Zen meditation. We can also have the spirit of zazen when we are doing things if we do them wholeheartedly.

Zen—Zen began in China and traveled from there to Korea, Japan, and around the world. It includes meditation, art, and a way of living and being.

zendo—The zendo is the hall in a Zen temple where people come together to meditate.

Bala Kids
An imprint of Shambhala Publications, Inc.
2129 13th Street
Boulder, Colorado 80302
www.shambhala.com

Cover art: Melissa Iwai
Design by Kara Plikaitis

9 8 7 6 5 4 3 2 1

First Edition
Printed in Singapore

Shambhala Publications makes every effort to print on acid-free,
recycled paper.
Bala Kids is distributed worldwide by Penguin Random House, Inc.,
and its subsidiaries.

Library of Congress Cataloging-in-Publication Data
Names: Burges, Laura, author. | Iwai, Melissa, illustrator.
Title: Zen for kids: 50+ mindful activities and stories to shine loving-
kindness in the world / Laura Burges; illustrated by Melissa Iwai.
Identifiers: LCCN 2021039088 | ISBN 9781611809923 (trade paperback)
Subjects: LCSH: Zen Buddhism—Juvenile literature. | Mindfulness
(Psychology)—Juvenile literature. | Zen meditations—Juvenile literature.
Classification: LCC BQ9265.7 .B87 2023 | DDC 294.3/927—dc23
LC record available at https://lccn.loc.gov/2021039088